VERBAL REASONING

(age 9-10)

SET 1

Multiple choice

Mary and Barbara Walsh M.A. (Oxon), P.G.C.E.

This book is intended to help familiarize children with the types of question they are likely to encounter in contemporary multiple choice verbal reasoning tests. However, in two papers, we have incorporated sections more usually found in standard version 11+ tests. One of these sections is in Test 1a, questions 53-59, where pupils are asked to arrange words in a logical order and identify which word is placed in the middle of the series. The second section is in Test 1c, questions 16-22, where pupils are asked to find the general word which describes the type of word the other vocabulary represents. We have chosen to omit the "dual meaning" style of question in these tests as this question type appears in our more advanced papers.

ISBN 978-0-9553099-3-9

Published by bumblebee (UK) Limited
Registered Office: 4 The Sanctuary, 23 Oakhill Grove, Surbiton, Surrey KT6 6DU

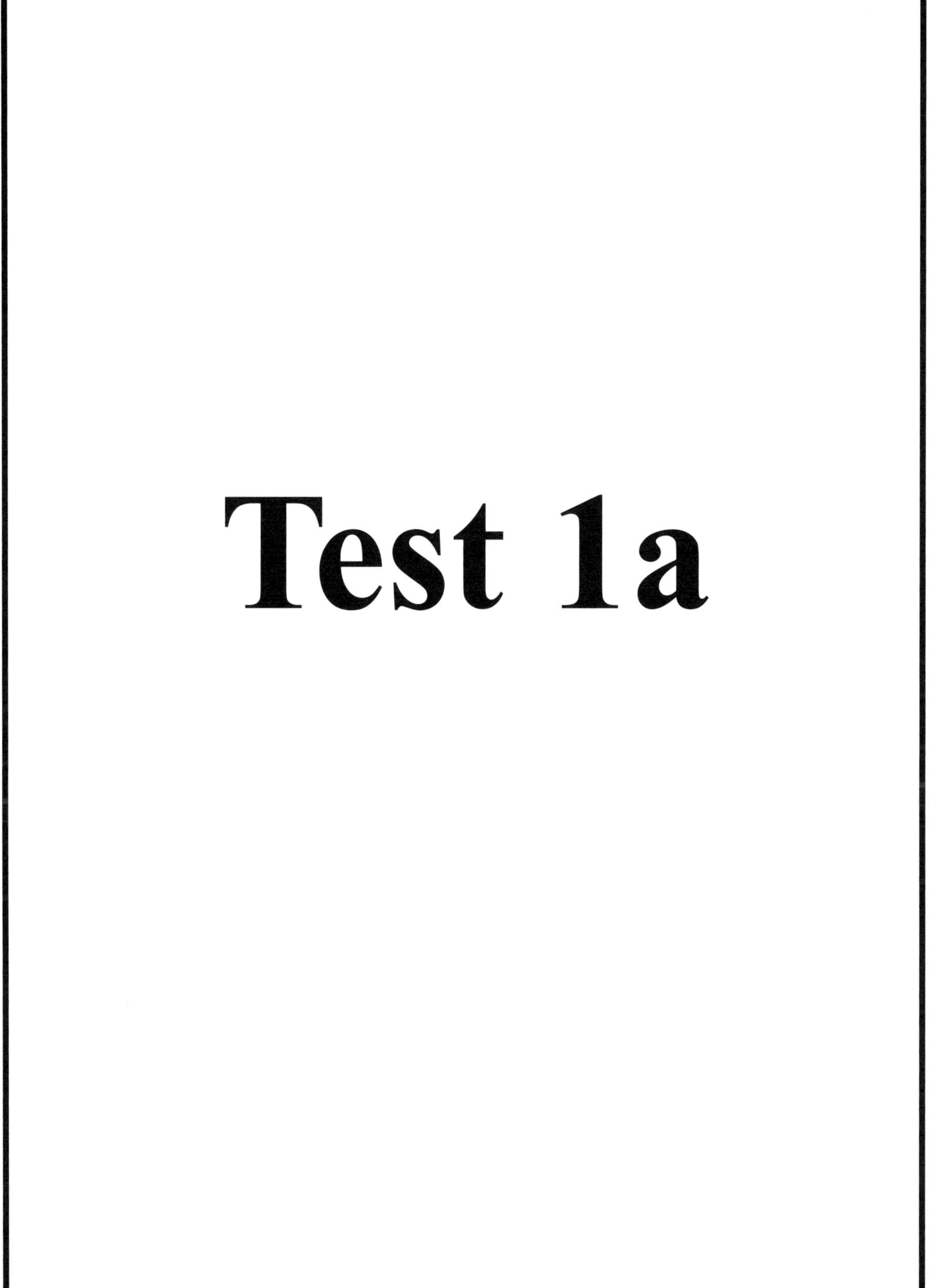

Test 1a

In the following questions, take a letter from the first word and move it into the second word to form two new words.

All the other letters must stay in the same order and both new words must make sense.

Work out which letter moves and mark it on the answer sheet.

Example

camel back

Answer

l (the two new words are **came** and **black**)

QUESTION **1**

clamp any

QUESTION **2**

cheap nice

QUESTION **3**

began ride

QUESTION **4**

grown cook

QUESTION **5**

cream past

QUESTION **6**

noise mad

QUESTION **7**

table super

KEEP GOING

In these questions, find a letter that will complete the word in front of the brackets and begin the word after the brackets. You must use the **same** letter in **both** sets of brackets.

Example

sin (?) ood
dra (?) oal

Answer

g (the four words are **sing, good, drag, goal**)

QUESTION **8**

be (?) urn
ma (?) ake

QUESTION **9**

kno (?) arn
dum (?) at

QUESTION **10**

fle (?) on
sa (?) ind

QUESTION **11**

are (?) ir
pum (?) rc

QUESTION **12**

oa (?) ill
dar (?) ite

QUESTION **13**

pe (?) loud
aren (?) im

QUESTION **14**

dra (?) ing
cla (?) ait

GO STRAIGHT ON

In these questions, letters represent numbers. Work out the answer to each sum, find its letter and mark it on the answer sheet.

Example

If A=2, B=3, C=4, D=6, E=12,

what is the answer to this sum **as a letter**?

C + D + A = [?]

Answer

E

QUESTION **15**

If A=3, B=4, C=5, D=8, E=12,

what is the answer to this sum **as a letter**?

A + B + C = [?]

QUESTION **16**

If A=2, B=3, C=10, D=15, E=20,

what is the answer to this sum **as a letter**?

D - B - A = [?]

QUESTION **17**

If A=2, B=3, C=4, D=6, E=7,

what is the answer to this sum **as a letter**?

A + E - B = [?]

QUESTION **18**

If A=2, B=3, C=4, D=24, E=30,

what is the answer to this sum **as a letter**?

B x C x A = [?]

KEEP GOING

QUESTION **19**

If A=2, B=6, C=10, D=12, E=18,

what is the answer to this sum **as a letter**?

E + B - C - A = [?]

QUESTION **20**

If A=1, B=2, C=6, D=12, E=24,

what is the answer to this sum **as a letter**?

E ÷ C ÷ B = [?]

QUESTION **21**

If A=3, B=4, C=6, D=7, E=14,

what is the answer to this sum **as a letter**?

E - C + A - B = [?]

Read the following information, then work out the correct answer to the question and mark its letter on the answer sheet.

QUESTION **22**

Dominic and his friends have Saturday jobs.
Dominic earns the most.
He earns £6.00 an hour.
It takes Julie three hours to earn as much as Dominic makes in one hour.
Per hour, Joe earns twice as much as Julie.

How many hours will Joe have to work to earn as much money as Dominic earns in two hours?

a. 1 ½ hours

b. 2 hours

c. 3 hours

d. 6 hours

e. 8 hours

GO STRAIGHT ON

In the following questions, find **two** words, one from each row, that are **most opposite in meaning.**

Example

(minute day hour)
(moon second night)

Answer

day night

QUESTION **23**

(arrival come airport)
(plane suitcase departure)

QUESTION **24**

(sad cowardly anxious)
(sly brave miserable)

QUESTION **25**

(cut leave join)
(away separate distance)

QUESTION **26**

(loose bet beat)
(gain win tight)

QUESTION **27**

(best worse better)
(poor worst good)

QUESTION **28**

(timid rude anxious)
(shy nervous bold)

QUESTION **29**

(always seldom never)
(annual sometimes often)

QUESTION **30**

(joy tears cry)
(happiness misery frown)

KEEP GOING

In the following series, find the number which comes next in the most sensible way, and mark it on the answer sheet.

Example

6 7 9 12 16 [?]

Answer

21

QUESTION **31**

6 9 12 15 18 [?]

QUESTION **32**

2 2 3 5 8 [?]

QUESTION **33**

5 8 6 10 7 12 [?]

QUESTION **34**

9 10 12 16 24 [?]

QUESTION **35**

15 20 27 36 47 [?]

QUESTION **36**

6 9 11 14 16 [?]

QUESTION **37**

8 16 11 22 17 [?]

GO STRAIGHT ON

In each sentence there is a word of **four** letters hidden between the end of one word and the beginning of the next.

Find the pair of words that contains the hidden word and mark your answer on the answer sheet.

Example

The athlete was determined to win.

Answer

The athlete (the hidden word is **heat**)

QUESTION **38**

How late will you be tonight?

QUESTION **39**

Chelsea lost the game on penalties.

QUESTION **40**

Do you live in this area?

QUESTION **41**

We asked for an extra ticket.

QUESTION **42**

Who lent you that computer game?

QUESTION **43**

Some pets can be hard work!

QUESTION **44**

He lost all sense of time.

KEEP GOING

Read the following information, then work out the correct answer to the question and mark it on the answer sheet.

QUESTION **45**

Carrots are more expensive than cabbage.
Broccoli costs more than mushrooms.
Peas cost less than mushrooms but more than carrots.

Which is the least expensive vegetable?

a. broccoli

b. carrots

c. peas

d. cabbage

e. mushrooms

GO STRAIGHT ON

In each of the following questions, there is the same relationship between the word outside the brackets and a word inside each set of brackets. Choose **two** words, one from each set of brackets, that complete the sentence in the best way.

Example

hat is to
(face scarf head)

as **shoe** is to
(toe foot leather)

Answer

head **foot**

QUESTION **46**

gold is to
(expensive jewel metal)

as **sapphire** is to
(ring blue stone)

QUESTION **47**

deep is to
(width shallow depth)

as **long** is to
(way length broad)

QUESTION **48**

square is to
(four octagon oval)

as **triangle** is to
(shape angle hexagon)

QUESTION **49**

pedestrian is to
(plane walk foot)

as **motorist** is to
(speed drive break)

KEEP GOING

QUESTION **50**

television is to
(remote viewer film)

as **radio** is to
(station car listener)

QUESTION **51**

hot is to
(flame cold sun)

as **boil** is to
(spot water freeze)

QUESTION **52**

optician is to
(feet hair eyes)

as **dentist** is to
(chair teeth drill)

GO STRAIGHT ON

In the following questions, arrange the words in a logical order and decide which word comes in the middle.
Mark this word on your answer sheet.

Example

cold hot boiling warm freezing

Answer

warm

QUESTION **53**

minute petite large average immense

QUESTION **54**

May February July April August

QUESTION **55**

sentence vowel chapter word paragraph

QUESTION **56**

week day second decade minute

QUESTION **57**

raindrop lake sea puddle ocean

QUESTION **58**

peach apricot grape pineapple mango

QUESTION **59**

forehead nose chin eyebrow mouth

KEEP GOING

A B C D E F G H I J K L M N O P Q R S T U V W X Y Z

The alphabet is here to help you with the following questions. Work out which letter or pair of letters will come next in the series and mark your answer on the answer sheet.

Example 1

R T V X **[Z]**

Example 2

DL GO JR MU **[PX]**

QUESTION **60**

B E H K N [?]

QUESTION **61**

Z X V T R [?]

QUESTION **62**

C E H L Q [?]

QUESTION **63**

JA LC NE PG RI [?]

QUESTION **64**

KN IL GJ EH CF [?]

QUESTION **65**

YJ VM SP PS MV [?]

QUESTION **66**

MR OM RI VF AD [?]

GO STRAIGHT ON

In the following questions, find **one** word from the top row and **one** word from the bottom row that will join together to form **one** correctly spelt new word. The order of the letters does not change.

The word from the top row always comes first.

Mark **both** words on the answer sheet.

Example

(rat pig dog)
(me her him)

Answer

rat **her** (the word is **rather**)

QUESTION **67**

(at be on)
(have own buy)

QUESTION **68**

(back arm leg)
(land soil ground)

QUESTION **69**

(bad fir for)
(jar tune sty)

QUESTION **70**

(mode way style)
(speed rate beat)

QUESTION **71**

(it men at)
(alien are ace)

QUESTION **72**

(use butter ice)
(cup mug full)

QUESTION **73**

(sore pain scar)
(some let tan)

KEEP GOING

The word in brackets in the top row has been formed using the letters from the two words on either side.
Find the missing word in the second row that has been formed in the **same way** and mark your answer on the sheet.

Example

pint (pain) bean
soap (?) salt

Answer

slot

QUESTION **74**

first (star) table
mitre (?) enter

QUESTION **75**

pale (reap) rote
rate (?) pine

QUESTION **76**

power (worn) clown
digit (?) plane

QUESTION **77**

bride (idea) stair
spoon (?) agent

QUESTION **78**

rusty (rye) stare
ghoul (?) leafy

QUESTION **79**

tear (hear) than
sail (?) area

QUESTION **80**

match (team) heart
error (?) buddy

END OF TEST 1a

Test 1b

In the following questions, find **one** word from the top row and **one** word from the bottom row that will join together to form **one** correctly spelt new word.
The order of the letters does not change.

The word from the top row always comes first.

Mark **both** words on the answer sheet.

Example

(rat pig dog)
(me her him)

Answer

rat **her** (the word is **rather**)

QUESTION **1**

(neck ear hand)
(some many all)

QUESTION **2**

(hat rug but)
(on at by)

QUESTION **3**

(in at of)
(one ten salt)

QUESTION **4**

(fog mess mist)
(age sure take)

QUESTION **5**

(bud mist log)
(rust red din)

QUESTION **6**

(is arm has)
(soil land any)

QUESTION **7**

(be am are)
(over hide low)

KEEP GOING

In the following questions, take a letter from the first word and move it into the second word to form two new words.

All the other letters must stay in the same order and both new words must make sense.

Work out which letter moves and mark it on the answer sheet.

Example

camel back

Answer

l (the two new words are **came** and **black**)

QUESTION **8**

peach stale

QUESTION **9**

shore eight

QUESTION **10**

break steam

QUESTION **11**

range meat

QUESTION **12**

canoe lot

QUESTION **13**

chair fat

QUESTION **14**

heard cram

GO STRAIGHT ON

MULTIPLE CHOICE ANSWER SHEET 1a

Please mark your answers with a single line from side to side across the box

Do not mark outside the boxes

EXAMPLE	1	2	3	4	5	6	7
c	c	c	b	g	c	n	t
a	l	h	e	r	r	o	a
m	a	e	g	o	e	i	b
e	m	a	a	w	a	s	l
l (marked)	p	p	n	n	m	e	e

EXAMPLE	8	9	10	11	12	13	14
w	b	b	a	a	k	a	b
t	d	d	d	d	m	c	g
m	g	e	e	e	n	e	p
k	t	t	m	m	r	g	t
g (marked)	w	w	w	o	s	p	w

EXAMPLE	15	16	17	18	19	20	21	22
A	A	A	A	A	A	A	A	A
B	B	B	B	B	B	B	B	B
C	C	C	C	C	C	C	C	C
D	D	D	D	D	D	D	D	D
E (marked)	E	E	E	E	E	E	E	E

EXAMPLE

minute	moon
day (marked)	second
hour	night (marked)

23

arrival	plane
come	suitcase
airport	departure

24

sad	sly
cowardly	brave
anxious	miserable

25

cut	away
leave	separate
join	distance

26

loose	gain
bet	win
beat	tight

27

best	poor
worse	worst
better	good

28

timid	shy
rude	nervous
anxious	bold

29

always	annual
seldom	sometimes
never	often

30

joy	happiness
tears	misery
cry	frown

EXAMPLE	31	32	33	34	35	36	37
19	20	12	8	28	56	17	19
20	21	13	10	30	58	18	21
21 (marked)	22	14	12	32	59	19	22
22	23	15	14	38	60	20	34
25	24	17	16	40	61	21	36

PLEASE TURN OVER THE PAGE

EXAMPLE	38	39	40	41
The athlete	How late	Chelsea lost	Do you	We asked
athlete was	late will	lost the	you live	asked for
was determined	will you	the game	live in	for an
determined to	you be	game on	in this	an extra
to win.	be tonight?	on penalties.	this area?	extra ticket.

42	43	44	45
Who lent	Some pets	He lost	a
lent you	pets can	lost all	b
you that	can be	all sense	c
that computer	be hard	sense of	d
computer game?	hard work!	of time.	e

EXAMPLE		46		47		48	
face	toe	expensive	ring	width	way	four	shape
scarf	foot	jewel	blue	shallow	length	octagon	angle
head	leather	metal	stone	depth	broad	oval	hexagon

49		50		51		52	
plane	speed	remote	station	flame	spot	feet	chair
walk	drive	viewer	car	cold	water	hair	teeth
foot	break	film	listener	sun	freeze	eyes	drill

EXAMPLE	53	54	55	56	57	58	59
cold	minute	May	sentence	week	raindrop	peach	forehead
hot	petite	February	vowel	day	lake	apricot	nose
boiling	large	July	chapter	second	sea	grape	chin
warm	average	April	word	decade	puddle	pineapple	eyebrow
freezing	immense	August	paragraph	minute	ocean	mango	mouth

60	61	62	63	64	65	66
O	O	T	SK	AC	JX	FB
P	P	U	TJ	AD	JY	FC
Q	Q	V	TK	BC	JZ	GA
R	R	W	UK	BD	KW	GB
S	S	X	VJ	ZC	KX	GC

EXAMPLE		67		68		69	
rat	me	at	have	back	land	bad	jar
pig	her	be	own	arm	soil	fir	tune
dog	him	on	buy	leg	ground	for	sty

70		71		72		73	
mode	speed	it	alien	use	cup	sore	some
way	rate	men	are	butter	mug	pain	let
style	beat	at	ace	ice	full	scar	tan

EXAMPLE	74	75	76	77	78	79	80
slap	mint	pear	gail	none	elf	rail	robe
slat	rant	peat	gain	nose	fey	rare	rode
slot	rein	peep	gale	note	fly	real	ruby
spat	rent	peer	gape	page	fog	rise	rude
spot	tent	pier	gate	poet	gay	sale	your

END OF TEST 1a

MULTIPLE CHOICE ANSWER SHEET 1b

Please mark your answers with a single line from side to side across the box

Do not mark outside the boxes

EXAMPLE
rat [marked] | me
pig | her [marked]
dog | him

1
neck | some
ear | many
hand | all

2
hat | on
rug | at
but | by

3
in | one
at | ten
of | salt

4
fog | age
mess | sure
mist | take

5
bud | rust
mist | red
log | din

6
is | soil
arm | land
has | any

7
be | over
am | hide
are | low

EXAMPLE	8	9	10	11	12	13	14
c	p	s	b	r	c	c	h
a	e	h	r	a	a	h	e
m	a	o	e	n	n	a	a
e	c	r	a	g	o	i	r
l [marked]	h	e	k	e	e	r	d

EXAMPLE	15	16	17	18	19	20	21	22
A	A	A	A	A	A	A	A	a
B	B	B	B	B	B	B	B	b
C	C	C	C	C	C	C	C	c
D	D	D	D	D	D	D	D	d
E [marked]	E	E	E	E	E	E	E	e

EXAMPLE	23	24	25	26
The athlete [marked]	She was	My broken	She painted	She loves
athlete was	was happy	broken ankle	painted happily	loves maths
was determined	happy to	ankle aches	happily on	maths most
determined to	to get	aches so	on her	most of
to win.	get home.	so much.	her own.	of all.

27	28	29	30
Do not	She begged	The war	The argument
not give	begged her	war made	argument continued
give me	her captors	made many	continued for
me your	captors for	many people	for several
your germs!	for mercy.	people homeless.	several days.

EXAMPLE	31	32	33	34	35	36	37
blue	moan	column	tennis	wound	walrus	furry	above
colour [marked]	weep	comic	football	plaster	tuna	soft	beneath
red	grumble	newspaper	skating	hurt	seal	rage	over
bright [marked]	complain	page	athletics	bandage	sardine	fury	below
yellow	cry	magazine	cricket	injure	salmon	anger	under

PLEASE TURN OVER THE PAGE

EXAMPLE

soft		fast	
easy	■	simple	■
gentle		pure	

38

cry	smile
happy	cheerful
laugh	sad

39

parcel	carton
bag	present
box	tube

40

stay	come
leave	remain
go	left

41

outlaw	prison
robber	thief
convict	judge

42

lazy	fancy
beautiful	idle
plain	dull

43

mystery	wizard
murder	puzzle
magic	chance

44

fortunate	happy
sad	lucky
poor	rich

45

dash	pile
heap	dawdle
rush	slow

EXAMPLE	46	47	48	49	50	51	52	53
5	48	61	16	63	32	6	3	a
6	52	63	17	64	35	7	10	b
7 ■	54	67	18	66	39	8	39	c
8	55	68	19	72	43	10	180	d
9	63	70	20	84	45	12	270	e

EXAMPLE	54	55	56	57	58	59	60
EAR	AGE	ADO	DIN	RAM	CUT	AIR	AND
HIP	ANT	ATE	LET	RIM	HAT	ARE	ARE
LAP	EEL	LOT	RAT	RUB	HIT	ARM	EAR
LIP ■	LOW	MAD	RED	RUM	HUT	ASH	EGG
NAP	OAR	MEN	RID	URN	KIT	EEL	END

EXAMPLE	61	62	63	64	65	66	67
pant	he	the	deck	lass	bent	acre	sale
part	ho	thy	dice	last	bone	dare	same
pray	oh	toe	iced	lose	none	dead	seal
trap	or	toy	wick	lost	note	race	seam
tray ■	so	try	wide	lots	tone	read	slam

EXAMPLE	68	69	70	71	72	73	74
OS	GH	MP	NZ	ARC	BD	FT	FM
OT	GI	OL	OY	ASC	BE	FU	FU
PW	HH	OM	OZ	ASE	BF	GT	GU
PX ■	HI	PL	PY	AVE	BU	GU	PI
QY	JI	PM	PZ	AYC	BV	HU	PV

75	76	77	78	79	80
5114	PARSE	25641	DEAD	2312	231234
5132	REAPS	34652	DEAR	2314	231434
5164	SPARE	36252	DEED	2332	243125
5632	SPEAR	41652	READ	4312	431234
5641	WASPS	56421	REAR	4314	432234

END OF TEST 1b

MULTIPLE CHOICE ANSWER SHEET 1c

Please mark your answers with a single line from side to side across the box

Do not mark outside the boxes

EXAMPLE
The athlete
athlete was
was determined
determined to
to win

1
The boys
boys ignored
ignored their
their parents'
parents' warning.

2
We shall
shall order
order Chinese
Chinese food
food tonight.

3
All the
the arrangements
arrangements have
have been
been made.

4
He travels
travels all
all over
over the
the world.

5
We will
will move
move in
in next
next April.

6
She was
was prepared
prepared for
for bad
bad news.

7
The girls
girls wanted
wanted to
to play
play football.

8
a
b
c
d
e

EXAMPLE: w, t, m, k, g

9: d, m, p, s, y

10: b, e, g, m, t

11: m, p, s, w, y

12: b, d, p, t, w

13: b, d, e, t, y

14: b, d, f, n, t

15: b, d, g, t, y

EXAMPLE: elm, oak, sycamore, tree, maple

16: bowl, dish, plate, crockery, cup

17: tulip, daffodil, crocus, flower, poppy

18: truck, van, vehicle, car, motorbike

19: pliers, spanner, screwdriver, tool, hammer

20: bracelet, necklace, pendant, jewellery, ring

21: barley, crop, oat, wheat, maize

22: sugar, ingredient, butter, flour, milk

EXAMPLE: soft, easy, gentle | fast, simple, pure

23: occur, disaster, time | event, happen, place

24: tired, entertain, bore | funny, amuse, awake

25: food, beverage, coffee | drink, tea, supper

26: agree, scorn, quarrel | squabble, hit, debate

27: astonishment, fear, birthday | agony, celebrate, surprise

28: praise, rejoice, grumble | refuse, complain, decline

29: enthusiastic, happy, clever | dull, delight, keen

EXAMPLE: EAR, HIP, LAP, LIP, NAP

30: DEN, RAG, RAT, RIG, RUG

31: AWE, EWE, HOW, OWE, WET

32: ACE, ERA, ICE, INK, ONE

33: BAN, BIN, BUN, MAN, MEN

34: BAR, CAR, DIE, ERA, IMP

35: AIR, AND, ARE, ARM, ROW

36: ARE, ATE, OAR, ORE, RAN

PLEASE TURN OVER THE PAGE

EXAMPLE
- pant
- part
- pray
- trap
- tray [x]

37 leap, pale, plea, real, reap

38 abet, bate, beat, byte, tube

39 den, doe, dog, don, log

40 chap, char, chat, clad, clap

41 bark, dare, dark, mare, mark

42 met, tie, toe, tot, vet

43 gate, gnat, rage, rant, rate

EXAMPLE
- rat [x] | me
- pig | her [x]
- dog | him

44 van, bus, car | pit, pet, put

45 beg, ask, plea | sure, king, get

46 guard, mode, way | pen, den, sty

47 see, look, sea | sun, son, sin

48 pull, tug, tear | in, on, over

49 mate, friend, pal | ship, boat, raft

50 cap, hat, head | can, able, will

51 so, or, us | full, kid, bit

EXAMPLE
- 19
- 20
- 21 [x]
- 22
- 25

52 16, 17, 18, 19, 20

53 0, 1, 2, 3, 4

54 27, 28, 29, 30, 31

55 0, 1, 2, 3, 4

56 6, 7, 8, 12, 13

57 0, 1, 2, 3, 4

58 48, 96, 100, 110, 120

EXAMPLE
- blue
- colour [x]
- red
- bright [x]
- yellow

59 eyes, nose, knee, lips, shin

60 triangle, diamond, oval, rectangle, circle

61 sleigh, car, moped, toboggan, lorry

62 aunt, daughter, cousin, mother, baby

63 mistake, correct, error, change, fault

64 water, juice, butter, wine, cake

65 optician, hero, victim, dentist, surgeon

66 chair, oven, table, wardrobe, carpet

67 a, b, c, d, e

EXAMPLE
- FOOD
- FOOL
- HOOD
- HOOP
- HOPE [x]

68 SHLY, SHMX, UJNY, UJOY, UJOZ

69 BAG, BIG, BOG, DIG, DOG

70 QHMF, QHNE, QHNG, SJOH, SJOI

71 PAT, PET, PIT, POT, PUT

72 CBA, CBZ, IHA, IHE, IHG

73 BAY, BOY, COY, DAY, TOY

---

74 FMLA, FMLZ, FNNC, HQQH, HQRH

75 DARE, DART, DATE, TART, TEAR

76 1354, 2352, 2435, 1324, 1352

77 13541, 15431, 25314, 25431, 25432

78 LEAP, MEAL, PALE, PALM, PEAL

79 1, 2, 3, 4, 5

80 3154, 3521, 5142, 5143, 5213

END OF TEST 1c

MULTIPLE CHOICE ANSWER SHEET 1d

Please mark your answers with a single line from side to side across the box

Do not mark outside the boxes

EXAMPLE: c, a, m, e, l (marked: l)

1: w, h, o, l, e

2: s, h, o, u, t

3: c, h, a, r, t

4: s, h, a, m, e

5: c, l, i, m, b

6: b, r, e, a, d

7: t, r, a, i, l

EXAMPLE: w, t, m, k, g (marked: g)

8: b, d, g, p, t

9: b, d, f, g, m

10: b, d, f, m, t

11: b, e, f, k, p

12: d, f, m, n, t

13: b, e, s, t, y

14: e, o, s, t, y

15: c, d, g, k, t

EXAMPLE: DQ, DR, EO, EQ, ER (marked: ER)

16: BC, BE, BF, CE, CF

17: ML, MS, MT, QS, QT

18: AW, AX, QN, QX, ZX

19: CM, DM, DS, FM, XS

20: NO, NU, ON, TO, TU

21: FG, GH, HG, HI, QR

22: CS, JR, KR, KS, KZ

23: a, b, c, d, e

EXAMPLE: EAR, HIP, LAP, LIP, NAP (marked: LIP)

24: PAN, PEN, PIN, POT, PUT

25: BIT, DON, HER, KID, THE

26: ACT, ART, LAG, LEG, PIN

27: TAN, TEN, TIN, TON, TUN

28: PAT, PET, PIT, POT, PUT

29: ATE, ACT, DON, KID, MAN

30: LAY, LIE, SIN, SON, SUN

31: a, b, c, d, e

EXAMPLE: face, scarf, head (marked: head) | toe, foot (marked: foot), leather

32: May, thirty, March | thirty-one, August, November

33: country, Africa, mountain | salt, sea, surf

34: valuable, rare, garden | enough, some, scarce

35: kayak, wood, liner | yacht, wind, water

36: cinema, film, watch | platform, actor, theatre

37: beach, hard, boulder | leaf, bud, branch

38: poor, prove, sad | money, rich, bank

PLEASE TURN OVER THE PAGE

EXAMPLE
FOOD
FOOL
HOOD
HOOP
HOPE

39
MAD
MAN
MET
PAN
PEN

40
OKTL
OMVN
QLVN
QMVM
QMVN

41
LED
LEG
PIG
PIN
PIP

42
FQQN
FRRM
FRRN
ZLLF
ZLLH

43
BEAD
BEAM
BEAN
BEAR
BEAT

44
PDZC
QCZB
QDZC
SFBE
SGBF

45
SLAB
SLAM
SLAP
SLAT
SLAY

EXAMPLE
minute, day, hour, moon, second, night

46
fancy, clumsy, elegant, careless, ugly, graceful

47
serious, partly, wise, foolish, wisdom, folly

48
all, few, none, some, much, many

49
confirm, real, false, rumour, deny, conduct

50
neat, long, broad, narrow, tidy, wide

51
fresh, bread, modern, new, stale, dough

52
twilight, midnight, morning, noon, day, sun

EXAMPLE
21, 22, 24, 34, 42

53
1, 3, 4, 8, 12

54
57, 58, 59, 60, 63

55
1, 2, 3, 4, 5

56
2, 4, 6, 8, 12

57
3, 4, 5, 6, 7

58
22, 23, 24, 25, 26

59
3, 4, 6, 7, 8

EXAMPLE
blue, colour, red, bright, yellow

60
tiger, leopard, thrush, wren, puma

61
guitar, trumpet, banjo, trombone, harp

62
race, hurry, start, commence, begin

63
star, comet, rain, moon, hail

64
brick, concrete, wool, cotton, glass

65
sleep, exit, depart, doze, leave

66
roast, grill, serve, fry, eat

EXAMPLE
3, 13, 18, 21, 40

67
9, 10, 11, 12, 13

68
7, 8, 9, 10, 17

69
3, 11, 21, 28, 32

70
5, 6, 7, 30, 42

71
1, 7, 8, 10, 12

72
6, 7, 8, 14, 16

73
9, 20, 21, 24, 25

EXAMPLE
slap, slat, slot, spat, spot

74
ease, eats, star, stew, stir

75
male, malt, mane, mate, melt

76
blab, blag, brag, bran, brat

77
ace, arc, are, arm, awe

78
last, late, lest, tale, tall

79
balm, bale, bard, bare, beam

80
mad, map, mat, met, mop

END OF TEST 1d

In these questions, letters represent numbers. Work out the answer to each sum, find its letter and mark it on the answer sheet.

Example

If A=2, B=3, C=4, D=6, E=12,

what is the answer to this sum **as a letter**?

C + D + A = [?]

Answer

E

QUESTION **15**

If A=2, B=3, C=5, D=8, E=16,

what is the answer to this sum **as a letter**?

B + C + D = [?]

QUESTION **16**

If A=3, B=6, C=7, D=9, E=15,

what is the answer to this sum **as a letter**?

(C x A) - B = [?]

QUESTION **17**

If A=2, B=4, C=8, D=10, E=12,

what is the answer to this sum **as a letter**?

(E ÷ B) x B = [?]

QUESTION **18**

If A=0, B=1, C=2, D=3, E=9,

what is the answer to this sum **as a letter**?

E ÷ D ÷ B = [?]

KEEP GOING

QUESTION **19**

If A=3, B=4, C=8, D=12, E=16,

what is the answer to this sum **as a letter**?

(A x E) ÷ B = [?]

QUESTION **20**

If A=3, B=5, C=9, D=15, E=20,

what is the answer to this sum **as a letter**?

(C x B) ÷ A = [?]

QUESTION **21**

If A=3, B=9, C=15, D=21, E= 27,

what is the answer to this sum **as a letter**?

E - B - A = [?]

Read the following information, then work out the correct answer to the question and mark it on the answer sheet.

QUESTION **22**

In a quiz, Jonathon scored 15 points.
Susan scored 6 more than Henry.
Jonathon scored 7 more than Susan.

How many points did Henry have?

a. 15 points

b. 8 points

c. 4 points

d. 3 points

e. 2 points

GO STRAIGHT ON

In each sentence there is a word of **four** letters hidden between the end of one word and the beginning of the next.

Find the pair of words that contains the hidden word and mark your answer on the answer sheet.

Example
The athlete was determined to win.

Answer
The athlete (the hidden word is **heat**)

QUESTION **23**

She was happy to get home.

QUESTION **24**

My broken ankle aches so much.

QUESTION **25**

She painted happily on her own.

QUESTION **26**

She loves maths most of all.

QUESTION **27**

Do not give me your germs!

QUESTION **28**

She begged her captors for mercy.

QUESTION **29**

The war made many people homeless.

QUESTION **30**

The argument continued for several days.

KEEP GOING

In the following questions, three of the five words are related in some way.

Find the **two** words that do **not** go with these three and mark them **both** on the answer sheet.

Example

blue colour red bright yellow

Answer
colour **bright**

QUESTION **31**

moan weep grumble complain cry

QUESTION **32**

column comic newspaper page magazine

QUESTION **33**

tennis football skating athletics cricket

QUESTION **34**

wound plaster hurt bandage injure

QUESTION **35**

walrus tuna seal sardine salmon

QUESTION **36**

furry soft rage fury anger

QUESTION **37**

above beneath over below under

GO STRAIGHT ON

Find **two** words, **one** from the top row and **one** from the bottom row, that are **closest in meaning**.

Mark **both** words on the answer sheet.

Example

(soft easy gentle)
(fast simple pure)

Answer

easy **simple**

QUESTION **38**

(cry happy laugh)
(smile cheerful sad)

QUESTION **39**

(parcel bag box)
(carton present tube)

QUESTION **40**

(stay leave go)
(come remain left)

QUESTION **41**

(outlaw robber convict)
(prison thief judge)

QUESTION **42**

(lazy beautiful plain)
(fancy idle dull)

QUESTION **43**

(mystery murder magic)
(wizard puzzle chance)

QUESTION **44**

(fortunate sad poor)
(happy lucky rich)

QUESTION **45**

(dash heap rush)
(pile dawdle slow)

KEEP GOING

In the following questions, find the number that will complete the sum correctly and mark it on the answer sheet.

Example

6 + 4 - 3 = [?]

Answer

7

QUESTION **46**

(9 x 7) - 8 = [?]

QUESTION **47**

(7 x 8) + 5 = [?]

QUESTION **48**

(132 ÷ 11) + 6 = [?]

QUESTION **49**

(72 ÷ 6) x 6 = [?]

QUESTION **50**

(96 ÷ 3) + 11 = [?]

QUESTION **51**

(57 + 9) ÷ 11 = [?]

QUESTION **52**

18 - (5 x 3) = [?]

KEEP GOING

Read the following information, then work out the correct answer to the question and mark it on the answer sheet.

QUESTION **53**

Newton, Chew, Lingley, Barrow and Gower are towns.
Only Chew and Gower have tennis courts.
Only Newton and Barrow have rugby clubs.
Only Newton, Lingley and Gower do not have football pitches.

Which town lacks football pitches, rugby clubs and tennis courts?

a. Newton

b. Chew

c. Lingley

d. Barrow

e. Gower

GO STRAIGHT ON

In each of the following sentences, **three letters next to each other** have been removed from the word in capitals. These three letters make one correctly spelt word without changing their order. Find the missing three letter word and mark it on the answer sheet. The sentence must make sense.

Example

He **SPED** on a banana skin.

Answer

LIP (The word in capitals is **SLIPPED**)

QUESTION **54**

We could hear the lions **RING** from miles away.

QUESTION **55**

There were many china **ORNATS** on display.

QUESTION **56**

That house badly needs **DECOING**.

QUESTION **57**

The children enjoyed their **SCBLED** eggs.

QUESTION **58**

The **ARCECT** won a prize for his designs.

QUESTION **59**

The **WHOUSE** was full of stolen goods.

QUESTION **60**

Lottery numbers are chosen at **ROM**.

GO STRAIGHT ON

Each question below contains three pairs of words. Find the word that completes the last pair of words in the **same way** as the other two pairs.
Mark your answer on the answer sheet.

Example

(marvel veal) (called lead)
(pantry [?])

Answer **tray**

QUESTION **61**

(where we) (money my)
(horse [?])

QUESTION **62**

(hooray hay) (ragged red)
(theory [?])

QUESTION **63**

(dagger rage) (minted dine)
(wicked [?])

QUESTION **64**

(find fine) (call calm)
(loss [?])

QUESTION **65**

(barter rate) (sacred dare)
(bonnet [?])

QUESTION **66**

(robot boot) (later tear)
(cared [?])

QUESTION **67**

(relish hire) (street test)
(medals [?])

KEEP GOING

A B C D E F G H I J K L M N O P Q R S T U V W X Y Z

The alphabet is here to help you with the following questions.

Work out which letters will come next in the series and mark your answer on the answer sheet.

Example

DL GO JR MU [?]

Answer

PX

QUESTION **68**

XY ZA BC DE FG [?]

QUESTION **69**

YC WE UG SI QK [?]

QUESTION **70**

AK DN GQ JT MW [?]

QUESTION **71**

FXH EWG DVF CUE BTD [?]

QUESTION **72**

BR BC BS BD BT [?]

QUESTION **73**

VF UG SI PL LP [?]

QUESTION **74**

CR RK DS QJ ET [?]

GO STRAIGHT ON

Three of these four words are written in number code.

The codes are **not** written in the same order as the words and one of the codes is missing.

PAWS **PEWS** **PEAR** **PEER**

5164 **5132** **5632**

Work out the correct code for each word and answer the following questions.

Mark the correct answer on the answer sheet.

QUESTION **75**

What is the code for the word **PEER**?

QUESTION **76**

Which word has the number code **25164**?

QUESTION **77**

What is the code for the word **WRAPS**?

KEEP GOING

Three of these four words are written in number code.

The codes are **not** written in the same order as the words and one of the codes is missing.

DEAD **REAR** **DEED** **DEAR**

2314 **2312** **2332**

Work out the correct code for each word and answer the following questions.

Mark the correct answer on the answer sheet.

QUESTION **78**

Which word has the number code **4314**?

QUESTION **79**

What is the code for the word **DEAD**?

QUESTION **80**

What is the code for the word **READER**?

END OF TEST 1b

Test 1c

In each sentence there is a word of **four** letters hidden between the end of one word and the beginning of the next.

Find the pair of words that contains the hidden word and mark your answer on the answer sheet.

Example

The athlete was determined to win.

Answer

The athlete (the hidden word is **heat**)

QUESTION **1**

The boys ignored their parents' warning.

QUESTION **2**

We shall order Chinese food tonight.

QUESTION **3**

All the arrangements have been made.

QUESTION **4**

He travels all over the world.

QUESTION **5**

We will move in next April.

QUESTION **6**

She was prepared for bad news.

QUESTION **7**

The girls wanted to play football.

KEEP GOING

Read the following information, then work out the correct answer to the question and mark it on the answer sheet.

QUESTION **8**

Jason put 10p in the charity box.
Jordan put in twice as much as Ali.
Ali gave twice as much as Jason but half as much as Peter.
Jason donated half as much as George.

How much money did the boys put in the box?

a. £0.55

b. £1.00

c. £1.05

d. £1.30

e. £1.40

GO STRAIGHT ON

In these questions, find a letter that will complete the word in front of the brackets and begin the word after the brackets.
You must use the **same** letter in **both** sets of brackets.

Example

sin (?) ood
dra (?) oal

Answer

g (the four words are **sing, good, drag, goal**)

QUESTION **9**

tra (?) ort
hel (?) our

QUESTION **10**

glu (?) at
lin (?) arth

QUESTION **11**

cro (?) ain
cla (?) lay

QUESTION **12**

gna (?) rim
flee (?) rue

QUESTION **13**

we (?) one
lam (?) ell

QUESTION **14**

so (?) ear
ear (?) ail

QUESTION **15**

sta (?) our
an (?) es

KEEP GOING

In the following questions, find the **general** word and mark it on the answer sheet.
It is the word which tells us what type of thing the other words are.

Example

elm oak sycamore tree maple

Answer

tree

QUESTION **16**

bowl dish plate crockery cup

QUESTION **17**

tulip daffodil crocus flower poppy

QUESTION **18**

truck van vehicle car motorbike

QUESTION **19**

pliers spanner screwdriver tool hammer

QUESTION **20**

bracelet necklace pendant jewellery ring

QUESTION **21**

barley crop oat wheat maize

QUESTION **22**

sugar ingredient butter flour milk

GO STRAIGHT ON

Find **two** words, **one** from the top row and **one** from the bottom row, that are **closest in meaning**.

Mark **both** words on the answer sheet.

Example

(soft easy gentle)
(fast simple pure)

Answer

easy simple

QUESTION **23**

(occur disaster time)
(event happen place)

QUESTION **24**

(tired entertain bore)
(funny amuse awake)

QUESTION **25**

(food beverage coffee)
(drink tea supper)

QUESTION **26**

(agree scorn quarrel)
(squabble hit debate)

QUESTION **27**

(astonishment fear birthday)
(agony celebrate surprise)

QUESTION **28**

(praise rejoice grumble)
(refuse complain decline)

QUESTION **29**

(enthusiastic happy clever)
(dull delight keen)

KEEP GOING

In each of the following sentences, **three letters next to each other** have been removed from the word in capitals.
These three letters make one correctly spelt word without changing their order.
Find the missing three letter word and mark it on the answer sheet.
The sentence must make sense.

Example

He **SPED** on a banana skin.

Answer

LIP (The word in capitals is **SLIPPED**)

QUESTION **30**

Dad parked the car in the **GAE**.

QUESTION **31**

Rain **SERS** are forecast for today.

QUESTION **32**

My brother has just got his driving **LNCE**.

QUESTION **33**

The car was **ADONED** by the side of the road.

QUESTION **34**

Our team has **ROVED** dramatically this season.

QUESTION **35**

The students began to think about their future **CERS**.

QUESTION **36**

Snakes and Ladders is a type of **BD** game.

GO STRAIGHT ON

Each question below contains three pairs of words. Find the word that completes the last pair of words in the **same way** as the other two pairs.

Mark your answer on the answer sheet.

Example

(marvel veal) (called lead)
(pantry [?])

Answer

tray

QUESTION **37**

(steam mate) (hates seat)
(paler [?])

QUESTION **38**

(talked tale) (pollen pole)
(beauty [?])

QUESTION **39**

(rabbit bar) (talent eat)
(golden [?])

QUESTION **40**

(sort shot) (want what)
(camp [?])

QUESTION **41**

(vine wine) (sent tent)
(lark [?])

QUESTION **42**

(pastry sty) (league age)
(motive [?])

QUESTION **43**

(cricket rice) (thanked hate)
(granted [?])

KEEP GOING

In the following questions, find **one** word from the top row and **one** word from the bottom row that will join together to form **one** correctly spelt new word.
The word from the top row always comes first.
Mark **both** words on the answer sheet.

Example

(rat pig dog)
(me her him)

Answer

rat **her** (the word is **rather**)

QUESTION **44**

(van bus car)
(pit pet put)

QUESTION **45**

(beg ask plea)
(sure king get)

QUESTION **46**

(guard mode way)
(pen den sty)

QUESTION **47**

(see look sea)
(sun son sin)

QUESTION **48**

(pull tug tear)
(in on over)

QUESTION **49**

(mate friend pal)
(ship boat raft)

QUESTION **50**

(cap hat head)
(can able will)

QUESTION **51**

(so or us)
(full kid bit)

GO STRAIGHT ON

In the following series, find the number which comes next in the most sensible way, and mark it on your answer sheet.

Example

6 7 9 12 16 [?]

Answer

21

QUESTION **52**

3 4 6 9 13 [?]

QUESTION **53**

15 10 6 3 1 [?]

QUESTION **54**

4 7 11 16 22 [?]

QUESTION **55**

23 17 12 8 5 [?]

QUESTION **56**

5 7 6 9 7 11 [?]

QUESTION **57**

36 25 16 9 4 [?]

QUESTION **58**

1 1 2 6 24 [?]

KEEP GOING

In the following questions, three of the five words are related in some way.

Find the **two** words that do not go with these three and mark them **both** on the answer sheet.

Example

blue colour red bright yellow

Answer

colour bright

QUESTION **59**

eyes nose knee lips shin

QUESTION **60**

triangle diamond oval rectangle circle

QUESTION **61**

sleigh car moped toboggan lorry

QUESTION **62**

aunt daughter cousin mother baby

QUESTION **63**

mistake correct error change fault

QUESTION **64**

water juice butter wine cake

QUESTION **65**

optician hero victim dentist surgeon

QUESTION **66**

chair oven table wardrobe carpet

GO STRAIGHT ON

Read the following information, then work out the correct answer to the question and mark it on the answer sheet.

QUESTION **67**

In a foreign language HOON GAT means large bowl and HOON TIG means small bowl.

If KARL GAT means large plate, how would you write small plate?

a. TIG KARL

b. KARL HOON

c. KARL TIG

d. HOON KARL

c. GAT HOON

GO STRAIGHT ON

A B C D E F G H I J K L M N O P Q R S T U V W X Y Z

The alphabet is here to help you with the following questions.
There is a different code for each question.
Find the correct answer and mark it on the answer sheet.

Example

If the code for **LOVE** is **KNUD**, what does **GNOD** mean?

Answer

HOPE

QUESTION **68**

If the code for **TALL** is **UBMM**, what is the code for **TINY**?

QUESTION **69**

If the code for **BAT** is **CBU**, what does **EPH** mean?

QUESTION **70**

If the code for **BEST** is **ADRS**, what is the code for **RING**?

QUESTION **71**

If the code for **RUG** is **TWI**, what does **RKV** mean?

QUESTION **72**

If the code for **SUM** is **PRJ**, what is the code for **FED**?

QUESTION **73**

If the code for **OLD** is **NKC**, what does **ANX** mean?

QUESTION **74**

If the code for **LUCK** is **MWFO**, what is the code for **GOOD**?

KEEP GOING

Three of these four words are written in number code.

The codes are **not** written in the same order as the words and one of the codes is missing.

DATE DART TART TEAR

1324 2435 2352

Work out the correct code for each word and answer the following questions.

Mark the correct answer on the answer sheet.

QUESTION **75**

Which word has the number code **1352**?

QUESTION **76**

Find the code for the word **DATE.**

QUESTION **77**

Find the code for the word **TREAT**.

KEEP GOING

Three of these four words are written in number code.

The codes are **not** written in the same order as the words and one of the codes is missing.

PALE PEAL MEAL LEAP

3152 4215 3215

Work out the correct code for each word and answer the following questions.

Mark the correct answer on the answer sheet.

QUESTION **78**

Which word has the number code **3152**?

QUESTION **79**

Find the number which represents the letter **M.**

QUESTION **80**

Find the code for the word **LAME.**

END OF TEST 1c

Test 1d

In the following questions, take a letter from the first word and move it into the second word to form two new words.

All the other letters must stay in the same order and both new words must make sense.

Work out which letter moves and mark it on the answer sheet.

Example

camel back

Answer

l (the two new words are **came** and **black**)

QUESTION **1**

whole tin

QUESTION **2**

shout cold

QUESTION **3**

chart tree

QUESTION **4**

shame tough

QUESTION **5**

climb sore

QUESTION **6**

bread sleep

QUESTION **7**

trail fail

KEEP GOING

In these questions, find a letter that will complete the word in front of the brackets and begin the word after the brackets. You must use the **same** letter in **both** sets of brackets.

Example

sin (?) ood
dra (?) oal

Answer

g (the four words are **sing, good, drag, goal**)

QUESTION **8**

fo (?) oat
bra (?) oal

QUESTION **9**

toa (?) ull
wor (?) ust

QUESTION **10**

ge (?) ake
crea (?) ean

QUESTION **11**

tom (?) eg
gra (?) right

QUESTION **12**

loa (?) ish
scar (?) ear

QUESTION **13**

deb (?) our
fac (?) rail

QUESTION **14**

fur (?) acht
pit (?) ear

QUESTION **15**

gran (?) are
prou (?) uty

GO STRAIGHT ON

A B C D E F G H I J K L M N O P Q R S T U V W X Y Z

The alphabet is here to help you with the following questions. Work out which pair of letters will come next in the sequence and mark your answer on the answer sheet.

Example

RB is to **TD**
as
CP is to [?]

Answer

ER

QUESTION **16**

PS is to **RU**
as
AD is to [?]

QUESTION **17**

CD is to **EH**
as
OP is to [?]

QUESTION **18**

PJ is to **UO**
as
VS is to [?]

QUESTION **19**

DE is to **GB**
as
AP is to [?]

QUESTION **20**

MN is to **JK**
as
QR is to [?]

KEEP GOING

QUESTION **21**

WT is to **RO**
as
LM is to [?]

QUESTION **22**

BP is to **FL**
as
GV is to [?]

Read the information below then work out the correct answer to the question.

Mark its letter on the answer sheet.

QUESTION **23**

A department store has four floors.
Cosmetics are sold two floors below the book section and one floor below electrical goods.
The shoe department is on the same floor as the books.
The toy department is two floors below the furniture department which is on the top floor.

What is sold on the ground floor?

a. toys

b. books

c. cosmetics

d. electrical goods

e. shoes

GO STRAIGHT ON

In each of the following sentences, **three letters next to each other** have been removed from the word in capitals.
These three letters make one correctly spelt word without changing their order.
Find the missing three letter word and mark it on the answer sheet.
The sentence must make sense.

Example

He **SPED** on a banana skin.

Answer

LIP (The word in capitals is **SLIPPED**)

QUESTION **24**

The **CARTER** made beautiful furniture.

QUESTION **25**

The friends waved goodbye to each **OR.**

QUESTION **26**

Listen to the crowd's **REION** when Arsenal score!

QUESTION **27**

Few people enjoy driving long **DISCES**.

QUESTION **28**

That child has a very good **APITE**!

QUESTION **29**

The **OR** often forgot his lines.

QUESTION **30**

The price he quoted seemed very **REAABLE**.

KEEP GOING

Read the information below then work out the correct answer to the question.

Mark its letter on the answer sheet.

QUESTION **31**

Amy, Lily, Oliver, Hal and Jake each have one pet.
One of them has a cat, three have rats and one has a snake.
Amy is older than Lily.
Hal, Jake and Amy are triplets.
Oliver is older than Amy.
The snake belongs to the oldest and the triplets have rats.

Who owns the cat?

a. Jake

b. Amy

c. Lily

d. Oliver

e. Hal

In each of the following questions, there is the same relationship between the word outside the brackets and a word inside each set of brackets. Choose **two** words, one from each set of brackets, that complete the sentence in the best way.

Example

hat is to
(face scarf head)

as **shoe** is to
(toe foot leather)

Answer

head **foot**

QUESTION **32**

April is to
(May thirty March)

as **September** is to
(thirty-one August November)

GO STRAIGHT ON

QUESTION **33**

continent is to
(country Africa mountain)

as **ocean** is to
(salt sea surf)

QUESTION **34**

common is to
(valuable rare garden)

as **plentiful** is to
(enough some scarce)

QUESTION **35**

paddle is to
(kayak wood liner)

as **sail** is to
(yacht wind water)

QUESTION **36**

screen is to
(cinema film watch)

as **stage** is to
(platform actor theatre)

QUESTION **37**

pebble is to
(beach hard boulder)

as **twig** is to
(leaf bud branch)

QUESTION **38**

poverty is to
(poor prove sad)

as **wealth** is to
(money rich bank)

GO STRAIGHT ON

A B C D E F G H I J K L M N O P Q R S T U V W X Y Z

The alphabet is here to help you with the following questions.
There is a different code for each question.
Find the correct answer and mark it on the answer sheet.

Example

If the code for **LOVE** is **KNUD**, what does **GNOD** mean?

Answer

HOPE

QUESTION **39**

If the code for **BAG** is **DCI**, what does **OCP** mean?

QUESTION **40**

If the code for **PEAR** is **QFBS**, what is the code for **PLUM**?

QUESTION **41**

If the code for **CAP** is **AYN**, what does **NGL** mean?

QUESTION **42**

If the code for **HAND** is **KDQG**, what is the code for **COOK**?

QUESTION **43**

If the code for **COME** is **EQOG**, what does **DGCV** mean?

QUESTION **44**

If the code for **BOOK** is **AMNI**, what is the code for **READ**?

QUESTION **45**

If the code for **TIDY** is **RGBW**, what does **QJYN** mean?

GO STRAIGHT ON

In the following questions, find **two** words, one from each row, that are **most opposite in meaning.**

Example

(minute day hour)
(moon second night)

Answer
day night

QUESTION **46**

(fancy clumsy elegant)
(careless ugly graceful)

QUESTION **47**

(serious partly wise)
(foolish wisdom folly)

QUESTION **48**

(all few none)
(some much many)

QUESTION **49**

(confirm real false)
(rumour deny conduct)

QUESTION **50**

(neat long broad)
(narrow tidy wide)

QUESTION **51**

(fresh bread modern)
(new stale dough)

QUESTION **52**

(twilight midnight morning)
(noon day sun)

KEEP GOING

In the following questions, find the number that will complete the sum correctly and mark it on the answer sheet.

Example

6 x 7 = 20 + [?]

Answer

22

QUESTION **53**

6 x 4 = 3 x [?]

QUESTION **54**

21 x 3 = 4 + [?]

QUESTION **55**

27 + 23 = 25 x [?]

QUESTION **56**

56 ÷ 7 = 2 x [?]

QUESTION **57**

19 + 17 = 6 x [?]

QUESTION **58**

41 - 16 = 50 - [?]

QUESTION **59**

22 - 5 + 7 = 3 x [?]

GO STRAIGHT ON

In the following questions, three of the five words are related in some way.

Find the **two** words that do not go with these three and mark them **both** on the answer sheet.

Example

blue colour red bright yellow

Answer

colour bright

QUESTION **60**

tiger leopard thrush wren puma

QUESTION **61**

guitar trumpet banjo trombone harp

QUESTION **62**

race hurry start commence begin

QUESTION **63**

star comet rain moon hail

QUESTION **64**

brick concrete wool cotton glass

QUESTION **65**

sleep exit depart doze leave

QUESTION **66**

roast grill serve fry eat

KEEP GOING

In the following questions, the three numbers in **each** group are related in the **same** way.

Find the number which belongs with the last group and mark it on the answer sheet.

Example

(6 [10] 4) (3 [15] 12)

(8 [?] 5)

Answer

13

QUESTION **67**

(8 [10] 2) (5 [9] 4)

(7 [?] 4)

QUESTION **68**

(12 [9] 3) (8 [6] 2)

(13 [?] 4)

QUESTION **69**

(3 [12] 4) (5 [25] 5)

(4 [?] 7)

QUESTION **70**

(16 [4] 4) (49 [7] 7)

(36 [?] 6)

QUESTION **71**

(7 [11] 3) (3 [13] 9)

(4 [?] 3)

GO STRAIGHT ON

QUESTION **72**

(6 [20] 4)   (5 [18] 4)

(5 [?] 2)

QUESTION **73**

(2 [9] 4)   (9 [55] 6)

(5 [?] 4)

KEEP GOING

The word in brackets in the top row has been formed using the letters from the two words on either side.
Find the missing word in the second row that has been formed in the **same way** and mark your answer on the sheet.

Example

pint	(pain)	bean
soap	(?)	salt

Answer

slot

QUESTION **74**

clove	(evil)	diced
write	(?)	raise

QUESTION **75**

poise	(soap)	opera
tramp	(?)	angel

QUESTION **76**

giggle	(glad)	larder
bubble	(?)	ragged

QUESTION **77**

clip	(ice)	lace
cram	(?)	warm

QUESTION **78**

alter	(real)	trail
legal	(?)	state

QUESTION **79**

heavy	(hive)	drive
berry	(?)	flame

QUESTION **80**

grape	(tag)	tight
leapt	(?)	modem

END OF TEST 1d

ANSWERS

PAPER 1a

1. m
2. e
3. g
4. r
5. e
6. i
7. b
8. t
9. b
10. w
11. a
12. k
13. a
14. w
15. E
16. C
17. D
18. D
19. D
20. B
21. D
22. C
23. arrival, departure
24. cowardly, brave
25. join, separate
26. loose, tight
27. best, worst
28. timid, bold
29. seldom, often
30. joy, misery
31. 21
32. 12
33. 8
34. 40
35. 60
36. 19
37. 34
38. How late
39. Chelsea lost
40. live in
41. an extra
42. Who lent
43. pets can
44. lost all
45. d
46. metal, stone
47. depth, length
48. octagon, hexagon
49. walk, drive
50. viewer, listener
51. cold, freeze
52. eyes, teeth
53. average
54. May
55. sentence
56. day
57. lake
58. peach
59. nose
60. Q
61. P
62. W
63. TK
64. AD
65. JY
66. GC
67. be have
68. back ground
69. for tune
70. mode rate
71. men ace
72. butter cup
73. scar let
74. rent
75. pear
76. gate
77. none
78. fly
79. rail
80. rude

PAPER 1b

1. hand some
2. rug by
3. of ten
4. mess age
5. mist rust
6. is land
7. be low
8. p
9. h
10. r
11. n
12. o
13. c
14. e
15. E
16. E
17. E
18. D
19. D
20. D
21. C
22. e
23. was happy
24. ankle aches
25. her own
26. of all
27. your germs
28. for mercy
29. war made
30. The argument
31. weep, cry
32. column, page
33. skating, athletics
34. plaster, bandage
35. walrus, seal
36. furry, soft
37. above, over
38. happy, cheerful
39. box, carton
40. stay, remain
41. robber, thief
42. lazy, idle
43. mystery, puzzle
44. fortunate, lucky
45. heap, pile
46. 55
47. 61
48. 18
49. 72
50. 43
51. 6
52. 3
53. c
54. OAR
55. MEN
56. RAT
57. RAM
58. HIT
59. ARE
60. AND
61. he
62. try
63. dice
64. lost
65. tone
66. read
67. same
68. HI
69. OM
70. PZ
71. ASC
72. BE
73. GU
74. PI
75. 5114
76. SPEAR
77. 34652
78. REAR
79. 2312
80. 431234

PAPER 1c

1. boys ignored
2. shall order
3. the arrangements
4. all over
5. move in
6. was prepared
7. girls wanted
8. d
9. p
10. e
11. p
12. t
13. b
14. n
15. y
16. crockery
17. flower
18. vehicle
19. tool
20. jewellery
21. crop
22. ingredient
23. occur, happen
24. entertain, amuse
25. beverage, drink
26. quarrel, squabble
27. astonishment, surprise
28. grumble, complain
29. enthusiastic, keen
30. RAG
31. HOW
32. ICE
33. BAN
34. IMP
35. ARE
36. OAR
37. real
38. beat
39. dog
40. chap
41. mark
42. tie
43. rage
44. car pet
45. plea sure
46. mode sty
47. sea son
48. pull over
49. friend ship
50. cap able
51. or bit
52. 18
53. 0
54. 29
55. 3
56. 8
57. 1
58. 120
59. knee, shin
60. oval, circle
61. sleigh, toboggan
62. cousin, baby
63. correct, change
64. butter, cake
65. hero, victim
66. oven, carpet
67. c
68. UJOZ
69. DOG
70. QHMF
71. PIT
72. CBA
73. BOY
74. HQRH
75. DART
76. 1324
77. 25432
78. PALE
79. 4
80. 5142

PAPER 1d

1. w
2. u
3. h
4. h
5. c
6. a
7. r
8. g
9. d
10. m
11. b
12. f
13. t
14. y
15. d
16. CF
17. QT
18. AX
19. DM
20. NO
21. GH
22. KR
23. c
24. PEN
25. THE
26. ACT
27. TAN
28. PET
29. ACT
30. SON
31. c
32. March, August
33. country, sea
34. rare, scarce
35. kayak, yacht
36. cinema, theatre
37. boulder, branch
38. poor, rich
39. MAN
40. QMVN
41. PIN
42. FRRN
43. BEAT
44. QCZB
45. SLAP
46. clumsy, graceful
47. wise, foolish
48. few, many
49. confirm, deny
50. broad, narrow
51. fresh, stale
52. midnight, noon
53. 8
54. 59
55. 2
56. 4
57. 6
58. 25
59. 8
60. thrush, wren
61. trumpet, trombone
62. race, hurry
63. rain, hail
64. wool, cotton
65. sleep, doze
66. serve, eat
67. 11
68. 9
69. 28
70. 6
71. 8
72. 14
73. 21
74. star
75. malt
76. brag
77. arm
78. tale
79. bare
80. mad